24 Pages and other poems

~ ~

Wave Books Seattle and New York

~ ~

~ ~

24 Pages and other poems

LISA FISHMAN

~ ~

Published by Wave Books

www.wavepoetry.com

Copyright © 2015 by Lisa Fishman

Wave Books titles are distributed to the trade by

Consortium Book Sales and Distribution

Phone: 800-283-3572 / SAN 631-760x

Library of Congress Cataloging-in-Publication Data

Fishman, Lisa, 1966–

[Poems. Selections]

24 pages and other poems / Lisa Fishman. — First edition.

pages ; cm

ISBN 978-1-940696-09-6 (limited edition hardcover) —

ISBN 978-1-940696-10-2 (trade pbk.)

I. Title.

PS3556.I814572A6 2015

811'.54—dc23

2014025625

Designed and composed by Quemadura

Printed in the United States of America

9 8 7 6 5 4 3 2 1

First Edition

Wave Books 048

The book was open, with its double

      shook / soot / look

It has no boots, is bare-

foot

      leaf-rhyme / tree-line

     oh and show how

a squirrel ate yellow flowers in the BAM-

                      BOO!

                stand on Blake Street,

                Berkeley

between house & fence

That the plant may leaf
out into leafing -- perhaps -- imprinted I heard
this pattern before
JUST LOOK

How many birds
in the eaves of a roof / if all the avenues in Avignon
were bridged by bridges then the song
could lengthen also

could be the sun
striking the ear -- JUST SO
the blank rabbit in the green field

Half the shoe
was stuffed with grass
why anyone are flown

The body be golden okay
plant onions to flower or wild grow
silent in face of it: fact
upon fact

What the yellow swallowtail eats has the wrong name:
prickly ash, neither prickly
nor ash, yet try
to posit as turning

the river the swimmer can
daylight, can current, can merge
in stead a form

Later the jewelweed goes in a bowl, turns in water
into its name -- gleams --
do not describe

How change it some
is synonym for love

How if it

served for chair for table & for bed

repair the ocean & the swath

But winter now and less repeats, in winter time of all the world

Was I said Clare a ball of grass / and what he meant by double tree /

    I saw the river

through my window once the leaves fell

& underneath was knowledge we did not dig up the lilies by the cat's fake

    grave

The lilies will die with the freeze / Ping the wild rabbit

eats at the cabbage seed / I write from town --

the wild rabbit is a town rabbit

for in the winter I live in town

& my own shadow all my company is not the case

& lone & see the shooting stars appear

said Clare; I also

picked currants in July

Next morning plus two my father died

Forever there is nothing to say

The reason for others is to hear past words of the self   past the surface

of a person / is it different

"to wish with the eyes in order to see more distinctly"

"to hasten the almond tree, flowering early"

One eye can't see close, the other can't see far

& broad old cesspools glittered in the sun

was, in the actual poem, "broad old sexpools glittered in the sun"

emended by editors for the Carcanet Press

body of sonnets -- what he meant

by sexpools perhaps pursue

this winter in town where also Yahara was made up

to name the river to sound Indian

Uneven seeing resembles a night the water was black
except for snow and was, despite the snow, still moving
I was on that bridge in the previous century
having escaped being harmed many times -- luck is sheer
straight through to the other side
Did you write about your feelings on the bridge / yes it was night
I don't know where the others are except for here
One is a journal / kingcups grow
"& shut up green & open into gold"

Notebook entry #
"58. A remarkable figure of Sleep
        as a winged child supine on a lion's skin, sleeping on its great half
unfolded wing of black <u>obsidian</u> stone. One hand is lightly placed on a
horn, with which it might be supposed to call together its wandering
dreams, the horn of dreams, and in the other a seedy poppy. The hard-
ness of the stone does not permit the arriving of any great expression."

A craft of ash, Ash craft: "We didn't know there were people there."
some mothers and some pieces
the various roots

~

We watched a boat go in a cave
of azure   are you sure
about this yes I'm sure

The girl is curious and would like to speak

Would understand the sentence as a crescent, half in
grass clad half an other

Hollow
out the shell, the egg hard-
boiled as for traveling
& spoon-struck for the peeling back
~~collective and individual grief~~

Margaret are you

1) the equinox   2)

out of the well

a story-child falling into

the city under the country

gathers her <u>cloak</u> around her

a <u>cloth</u> for

spring and fall

A nest has formed in the outer eave, you mean ear

looking down at the river as through a speech

Next

greet the horse across the north fence

Bird-racket overhead, her tremor-response to sound

~~~ | ~~~ | ~~~ | ~~~ | ~~~ | ~~~ | ~~~ | ~~~ | ~~~ | ~~~ |

Electricity runs through a wire

       However,

try handing clover across

The cat's face / the fox's face / 6 rides 5 dollars in June

Arrange the furniture around the trees
in a confusion of time and face

The willowleaves turn the brightest green
not red or yellow
if that's a willow
outside your window
if it's October again

To ride in the serpent or microscope, unbutton your shoes

please

The cat and fox were one
illusion out the second-story window, straight across
into another second-story window, out of which the animal uncanny stared
    back

Holding a bird you find almost no body under the wings

The girl entered the room

To be a tree, an axe, a fish a swan what else
she gathered her costumes -- brown clothing other clothing
from dirty laundry at the foot of the bed and from a drawer

The shoulders begin the body

Just now the girl again for a missing long-sleeved   Sorry I said
about the suitcase in your way

The forest came
into the seen

Oak maple many many ever

At intervals
thin birches leaned against the other dark

They were a tale, leaning

As if a corridor

could open or the EAR's two missing

letters -- h e a r t -- e a r t h -- wherever

an animal pops up out of the water such as a hooded merganser

appeared to do a somersault diving under, not like a mallard more like a
    child

or a ball -- it didn't come up

until it did

~

The foot steps off

a rock or line

Have wild violets dandelions

all the grass shown up in welcome yes &c. they wrote

& have you
put a jam jar
around the jam
in the apricot sun
shine
who broke in
the night before
my levitation
down the street from an open
magnolia tree

A scarecrow grew night by night in the field
Only the cats knew
until the crows knew
because it was tall and wore clothes
(the clothes grew
as it grew)
but the grapes and apples got eaten
by deer, who did not know
because, strange to say, the scarecrow had hooves
They were fooled, thinking "deer," hearing it move

"The streem of lyf now droppeth on the chymbe"

    slight burn as of edges -- <u>songed</u>

Out in the boat what looming over
was a trouble to my day
                boy, row
                the cloak a shore
If
lay a lion-limb against me
If
we stop speaking now for a while

There was fire in the small ghost
paper boat
lit with a match let go in the mouth
of a river

There were women   in the river
kathy   lisa   taralie
the oddest makeshift bathingsuits
they seem more like a kingdom

Sun flew over

sunflower over
          the sentence ends in
Rome?
Rhyme
          more
time

sun jacket wearing
               the bee
                    lists into the morning-
                    glory
                    which grows up the side of the greenhouse
          a - b - c

Two hives fine out of four
Subtraction
precedes cursive at the pink-cloth'd table
Approaching, again, an election

                              arctic drilling temporarily delayed
Under the surface -- sun face

          a sentence

frayed

24 Pages

March – July, 2012

Hot air balloon festival down the road
last weekend and this
time too is another

What but the meadow had filled
so much it looked like snow, the cottony forms of plantlife
left the witchgrass and the ryegrass and the eyegrass

The frog kite flips over
itself
makes a loop
of itself

Recall tying a chair to a kite & sitting there
for it to fly

Migration patterns askew in the hot March
blue herons also pass over
the frog kite's tongue

Laughter thought her
out
Winter over
clothes put by
in the cedar trunk
first phallus popped up: asparagus
in the land of the rabbits
or is the body a plant
with nerves that are fern

I guessed at the German: *die Farben sind dunkel*
The father sings dumbly   (The colors are dark)

feather-father
the bones earth or trees

"Something interwoven, embroidered, literally applied to the figures 'overwrought' or 'written over' . . ."

the sun spells

Laurel & Prunus

lily-white turnip

The cat also gallops -- learned to run by watching the horse

Don't think of them as trees

Her body fit entirely inside his body

The wishing swept into a boat
the forest floor -- edge of the meadow and its forms'
dispersal: milkweed cottonwood everything

The sky is pink in immediate
traveling
All kinds of FLAT GLASS
over the railroad tracks
Light "falls"
in a sound's resemblance

To be making something in the driveway, be alive
You dropped a metal thing just now
that clatter
resistant to breaking

Magnolia up the road is "unincorporated"
over the cemetery, County Road A
Where are the bees
By the hives and the herb
spiral, rock spiral -- hidden

Blackcaps and sumac take over

Tractors were driven around the Capitol
In the uppermost branches
a flicker drums in
to the cambium layer
I heard this while coming
The news too down our spine

of bindweed
"<u>Leaves</u> alternate
<u>Flowers</u> axillary
<u>Bracts</u> paired, heart-shaped, ovate
<u>Calyx</u> of 5 overlapping . . .
<u>Corolla</u> bell-shaped to funnelform
                    Mid-May – September"

Ecstatic evergreens, <u>out of</u> the ground
over anyone
imprinted with pine debris
As far as the poem is concerned
nothing important happening

More of a blur
the kingfisher flew twice overhead
Red-headed cranes <u>walked</u> along
the river's edge
the river a cooking pot

Face-down on the flowered cloth
one could feel their "pulses grieving"
Just now from the barn: hammering
Lie still
the body a well

If you put an <u>e</u> in whisky
are you looking through a whisk-eye

Not just the fruit but the roots in danger
this hottest summer
the deer fit over

"and all at once the marsh face full of frog faces."
I let it appear

Electric Fry Pan booklet
I land here

The orchard full of blossoms
two to three months early

March heatwave followed by drought

Not for the faint of heart or the cavalier, translation
"The frog book by Shimpei Kusano—so very nice, so frog-green."

In their bodies some of the singing staying.

Bring the throat up into the throat
it sounded like
through a broken window
5 a.m. in Ohio
4 in Wisconsin
Don't know anyone in Ohio

Who is Cordelia
cannot heave my heart into my mouth
July 22
Olbrich conservatory releases butterflies by the thousands
What do you think of

Line it with slabs of bark
& mount in a shady spot
to make a butterfly box for winter
for the Clouded, the Dogface
the Cloudless Sulphur
Harvester, Hairstreak, Spring Azure
Tropical Snout, Melissa, Atlantis
Admirals & Sisters, Cloudywings
Common Sooty Wing
Sleepy Duskywing
Tawny-edged, Least, Fiery, Roadside
. . . more Grass Skippers
gradually
the woodworker's daughter

Entire space of the forearm

under the prose and she ran

deeper and deeper into the grain or grove of the wood

I want to include Taralie saying everything was included
Three of us on bikes, & she said it riding past

Two weeks ago we gleaned berries
James may remember
"Look with your hands not just your eyes"

I swim with
the person who taught me
his presence around me the water
Dear who asked about my father

What FM said was "the first bite of honey in the early morning"
as honey is a solid
and I in a dialogue note the rafters
are holding a chair, a painting, wooden boards across the rafters'
wooden boards, +
a cat's jumped onto them straight from the floor

We begin to hoard time in the mornings, my sister and I
the hottest July
"moderate drought" changed to "extreme drought"
We bought a machine to replace the scythe
We look for cleats to stick to the earth
Must press furiously
blade into spurge

Two gifts in the trees you were thinking
mood ring, spoon ring, kite string, winter boot
A place to put everything
the branch shook

Iridescent Sea Holly growing on the bridge
attracts iridescent wasps, the woman with a belt of trowels said .
Ghost-blue ghost silver-gray

The yellow house was <u>in</u> the river, reflected intact

& tasselated corn

There is seeing for as if another
"or of a night language"
set out

HEAD OF THE MEADOW in the shape of a word

flight   flight   flight   flight

            o story

                 or steer me

                        a life said

September 20 – 21, 2013

It would be better if we <u>were</u> outside -- Lisa, Tianna and Sam
on Friday afternoon on the second day of Fall, at 4:30
and all.

Whoever you are, what do you know?

Time flaws
and to me flew not one white goose
but upside down I saw it's good
the undersides of maple leaves
the ragged edges' dandelion leaves, surprised they're there
this far past summer

Sam & Tianna have left the room; I too

It seems there's a mouse in my sock

24 times
or 24 centers

in the Daoist body   what a coincidence
I read that yesterday

Brooke told me he's fine now
No reason for him to tell <u>me</u>, but I'll tell Charles anyway
in a dream last night

Think of the colors
there now in the canyon
and above it in the ridges
elegy is unintended

Amtrak, Orfordville, Riverhead

July – August, 2013

And where the
sun was not on
the water it had
been a while
and it changed

sky am clear
say come here
Crown Paper & Bag Co.
Paper Merchants

I became this
and I became that
said a word not secretly
uh oh my ear

and to the tenth

cluster of cranes as if a village: Sandhill
stepping along
the standing water in the soyfields, liking the pools

a story came
into the lune
moth found in a book
Ha! Another thing happened next.

Into the river a stone's throw
quiets the loss
"Distant -- Close" --
two of the categories

We make you up
out of the water, unowned

Whoever died in the morning
More to go

The peaches were stolen out of the trees
when the favorite aunt, Eleanor,
left her house to run errands
A pickup drove up to the 2 trees in the backyard & emptied them
one day in August, 1963

More stories are under the whales
but they don't stay in one place

You can blur what you hear

Miss Montréal
loved the young man with curls
That was my dad, conjuring her

bird tracks
thistle   Queen Anne's Lace
sage   poplar
buckwheat   wild carrot
"all the ways"   black suspenders

marsh grass
cattails   Oxygen
oak trees   Nitrogen
thistle   neon-green river
No. 1 Bop Shop

July full of thistle
This is a little
strange notebook to see through
the sumac   some coal cars

I thought Hammond came before Gary
Mercury follows Apollo
not really

SKYWAY TOLL BRIDGE
appears for an instant

What are the names of 2 things
rampion   trillium
Max and Kate, what's the next question

The girl and her telescope were left in the field
Star or planet or space debris
in the lower right corner of the lens -- flames they called
the squiggly lines   nothing I saw

The white thing gleaming on the ground just sat there.
Stark white, oval shaped, lamp-sized, brightly shining
approached by a person hands-first, crouched, no flashlight--
a mushroom, probably laughing.

The person was small
The girl at the back of the orchard taller
<u>Was</u> = <u>is</u> (Helena & James)

Helvetica Jane and the Acrobat
--must come back to

~

Juniper trees in the kitchen -- that is a while
to go the mouth hopes.
Nothing will fit
or not everything. Primarily, when you are tending
a person dying, you feel them enter the skin of your arms.
It's electrical energy in our words
page words, same as the night.

Helena slept in the orchard & James will join them tonight--
cousin & telescope, the cat about.

Night before market
no apples yet
but melons again
white-fleshed precede orange; Charentais yet to come

The log-shaped melon's Korean: Jewel-of-the-Sun
to be traded for bread
The end

Jonah found
a frog in the currants
thirsty, he said, so we flicked water on it
& it sat still   throat pulsing
bright-greener than the stem, feet spread, attached to the stem

Three people one frog thousands of currants
Bashō, anyone, why write it down

Riverhead marries the kingfisher's son
Riverhead Meadowhead succubus chime
Riverhead riven and held   three tries
to recall the lines dreamt & altered, swept outside
into the mullein
which Ann said Indians made into shoes
James said the owl is a baker's daughter
& Chuck called the yellow moth Blue
the day we sorted currants into cocktails: the 213
and the 1 - 2 - 3   No, it isn't
a good time to get the Dodge van from the shop right now
Leave me alone to stew

~

A turtle swam under
my boat in the river, a large one with petals
accompanying

-- deletions --
       am on a train again
thinking that Jeff Ford's potatoes turned yellow
due to lack of rain and that I forgot to tell him
after he fell off his bike--the baker broke his shoulder but we continue to
    trade
2 melons for a spelt loaf and so on
One asshole is talking loud
and the train's too cold

~

It's the August
sounds we meet in
"we" stretches out but this moment means one person & self
as if it were that
a few miles could wrap around
      Greenish yellow, rather, potato plants' leaves
in a dry spell, wilted over dry sunned dirt
Right now the grapes are beginning to look good, but we spit them out

James is at *Hamlet*

James is in Hong Kong -- the other James,

who lives in Nebraska, eating avocados

Twelve hours from now I'll be home

Still trying, the train track rounds a bend
as if Chicago emerges
in Willa Cather's novel, when the el took just as long
from Andersonville to downtown -- that was in 1894

What did the sun say
once to the nightjar
or did the whippoorwill
whistle
       Good thing
Too bad

I don't have kapha bones
but neither are they overly vata bones
according to Jerry, who gave me a blanket, dreamed after acupuncture
turned into the movie
-style flying carpet such as Douglas Fairbanks sat upon
traveling the stars

Fold over the spine for it shows how
a vertebra sits like a fossil
amid plantlife and ocean-
synovial fluid: <u>winzig</u> (tiny)
fern-like portions of nerves & capillaries
made me sure once
we're actually plants

Could be a stone's throw
from the whole truth

The worst stop on the line is Dee Road
the tape-recorded voice announcing it
has no dee-round silence in its sound
My house is empty except for what's in it
Henry's long arms
made Ann say, "those long arms"
in the orchard picking peaches

In a car the news would be on--
"the mourning news" I thought this morning

Multiple kingfishers
led down the Yahara   one by one   on the east bank
I didn't say the poplars'
leaves turn backward when they're blown
like disk-shaped silver paddles
Noise we thought was whitewater, nothing but a poplar

The crickets come forward

night being sound

in two permissions self said when

bodies in secret are made of words

thought to be "atoms" because we can't read them

this the experience bears out

nothing less real for it

hence the pulsing in their midst   when we are

in the midst of them   still unknown

& stars lie down you close your eyes
a place falls
out of a tree
      what place
you there beside the spring

a fact about my father:
setting up the blue trapeze

The permissions lie further back

"It's an octopus. Those are the arms. I wrote
my name. And I make fish all around the octopus."

Further back.

"a series of circumlocutions"

Yes Eros/being/method

She has her own hockey skates
there in the garden

Oh overwrite nothing just as a trembling
named what was happening -- tree doing
that in the actual
eye-of-things
once in a Greek poem
appears in another
also in Dante, <u>andante</u>, remember

the row-covers, gauzy, are perfect for tying

from tree to tree, transforming

farm to midsummer

Theater of Orchard

upcoming next summer

Now crickets are under
the day time sounds

I slept 'til 15 minutes to 1
then walked on gravel to help wake up
thru the soles of my feet

Also the bean plants'
blossoms are red, twined up the cedar posts
so hummingbirds see them
so they can drink them

In to the blossom
Thel returned screaming -- a Blake thing
Experience, story of--

"Three-dimensional affairs, they occupy space in ways that reorient the body toward typically overlooked physical contours . . . of a given environment."

I stole the mackerel
from Whole Foods, felt it laughing
in my backpack all day

Things in the center, acting

Wildfire wildflowers out

All about
habitat -- two rails on the riverbank
King & Sora
and a canary, loose from a house
Each rare
-ly seen

Rails hop more than fly, and they did
from stone to stone

Untroubled, bright yellow, the canary ate berries

The thinness is inside
birds, their bones

What can the matter, this matter, be

Not wealthy but feathered, the parents

Time to address you, whoever

a ski is a key

How oddly words looking

at other words look

as if in the mirror her painting kept winding

backward, my grandmother's, one of a river

S-curving through trees   --trees stop rhyming!

with everything

copper-colored

Coming back to the kayak from out of the lake
the body sprawls awkwardly
up & in

evading elegy

The mother massages the tentacles
of succulent aloe vera

Instructions are given emphatically this equals love
as how to choose a loaf of bread   father to daughter

Desert flower Shelley Charles

The deep sleep yields
rest for the misshapen eye

Now think.

"The page was folded into a proper dart."

A certain number of out-of-body experiences are likely not to be perceived
Have you noticed this in your travels?

One Sun Jewel today was very good, eaten in the Juliets & Jaune Flamme

Quickly a tightrope was fixed between
a birch forest and a castle

altering memory
vexing the matter

she comes to count the horses
in the wild mustard

he tumbles down the iris
mountain

other eye seeing they
ought to alight

quintillions of arrows under the eyelids
must first be removed from the quiver

if it were woven
        the spider is tipsy
how are you sleeping

like a radish in the cooling nights
the dirt is breathing all the time too

September 22, 2013

Who is summer
spring or other
face   the beets are overwhelming
can't possibly be pickled grilled or eaten
all through autumn   hardly a problem
in the large sense but it's in front of me,
chickens behind me -- Miss White Butt
wanders around all day unlike her sisters, who stay put.

Lots of things float in the air when you're looking   what are they
bits of things, it actually seems like
zillions of things in the bright sun
zipping around, both up from the ground and down
from the sky or wherever
& the white pine needles are tingling out

~

Notes

Sources of quoted lines and phrases are given in the order in which they appear in the poems.

p. 6   "to wish with the eyes in order to see more distinctly" and "to hasten the almond tree, flowering <u>early</u>"—Elizabeth Barrett Browning, marginalia in her Greek and Hebrew Bibles

          "& broad old cesspools [sexpools] glittered in the sun"—John Clare, *Northborough Sonnets*

p. 7   "& shut up green & open into gold"—ibid.

p. 8   "58. A remarkable figure of Sleep . . ."—P. B. Shelley, "Notes on Sculpture"

p. 16   "The streem of lyf now droppeth on the chymbe"—Chaucer, "The Reeve's Prologue," *The Canterbury Tales*

p. 25   "Something interwoven, embroidered . . ."—Jeffrey N. Cox, glossing "brede" in a note on Keats's "Ode on a Grecian Urn," in *Keats's Poetry and Prose*

p. 32   "<u>Leaves</u> alternate . . ."—Agricultural Research Service of USDA, *Common Weeds of the United States*, illustrated by Regina O. Hughes

p. 34   "pulses grieving"—Friederike Mayröcker, "auxiliary romanticism, etc.,"
Raving Language: Selected Poems 1946–2006, trans. Richard Dove

p. 36   "and all at once the marsh face full of frog faces."—Kusano Shimpei,
"Birthday Party," *frogs & others.*, trans. Cid Corman and Kamaike
Susumu

          "The frog book by Shimpei Kusano—so very nice, so frog-green."
—Lorine Niedecker, letter to Cid Corman, May 13, 1963, *"Between
Your House and Mine": The Letters of Lorine Niedecker to Cid Corman,
1960 to 1970*, ed. Lisa Pater Faranda

p. 41   "the first bite of honey in the early morning"—Mayröcker, "such snow
and bite and eye-dairy," *Raving Language*, trans. Dove

p. 43   "or of a night language"—Robert Duncan, "From a Notebook," *Fictive
Certainties*

p. 69   "a series of circumlocutions"—Ronald Johnson, *To Do As Adam Did*

p. 72   "Three-dimensional affairs . . ."—Helen Molesworth on Cecilia Vicuña's
weavings in *Dance/Draw* exhibition catalogue, Institute of Contempo-
rary Art, Boston

p. 76   "The page was folded into a proper dart."—Iris Murdoch, *The Sea, the
Sea*

Acknowledgments

I thank the editors of the following magazines for publishing some of these poems and portions of poems, many in earlier forms or with different titles as indicated below:

Blackhawk Island Poems 2012:
  From "24 Pages":
    ["and all at once the marsh face full of frog faces."]

Cannot Exist:
  The first half of "& have you" (as "For Robert Grenier")
  From "24 Pages":
    ["Iridescent Sea Holly growing on the bridge"]
    ["Magnolia up the road is 'unincorporated'"]
    ["What FM said was . . ."]

Court Green:
  The second half of "& have you" (as "Los Angeles, 2011")
  From "24 Pages":
    ["Bring the throat up into the throat"]
    ["Entire space of the forearm"]
    ["I want to include Taralie saying everything was included"]
    ["Line it with slabs of bark"]

jubilat:

"That the plant may leaf" (as "In Stead a Form")

"The cat's face / the fox's face / 6 rides 5 dollars in June" (as "Being in Place")

MAKE:

"Margaret are you"

From "24 Pages":

["Hot air balloon festival down the road"]

["The cat also gallops -- learned to run by watching the horse"]

["To be making something in the driveway, be alive"]

["What but the meadow had filled"]

OmniVerse:

From "24 Pages":

["Laughter thought her"]

["'Something interwoven . . .'"]

["The frog kite flips over"]

["Tractors were driven around the Capitol"]

Pinwheel:

From "Amtrak, Orfordville, Riverhead" (as "Riverhead, August 2013"):

["Now crickets are under"]

["she comes to count the horses"]

["The crickets come forward"]

["The deep sleep yields"]

["The permissions lie further back"]

Sawbuck:

"The streem of lyf now droppeth on the chymbe" (as "Chime")

They Will Sew the Blue Sail:

From "24 Pages":

["Two gifts in the trees you were thinking"]

Volt:

"A scarecrow grew night by night in the field"

"Holding a bird you find almost no body under the wings"

"Sun flew over"

"The book was open, with its double"

"A scarecrow grew night by night in the field" was anthologized in *Best American Experimental Writing 2014* (Richmond, CA: Omnidawn).

Woodland Pattern Book Center, Milwaukee, published a broadside of "The book was open, with its double"; I'm grateful to Chuck Stebelton.

Portions of "24 Pages" were embroidered by Ann Engelman onto a memory cloth and exhibited in the 2014 Mary Hoard Art Show, Fort Atkinson.

I'm grateful to Ann Engelman, Amy Lutzke, and the Friends of Lorine Niedecker for a month-long residency on Blackhawk Island and Fort Atkinson as Lorine Niedecker Poet-in-Residence. Although most of the foregoing poems were written prior to that residency in November, 2012, the time helped me shape this collection.

~

This book is for Nicole Wilson, in memory of my father, Lionel Fishman (March 10, 1930 – July 22, 2010).